We All Need Food

Katie Peters

GRL Consultant Diane Craig,
Certified Literacy Specialist

Lerner Publications ◆ Minneapolis

Note from a GRL Consultant
This Pull Ahead leveled book has been carefully designed for beginning readers.
A team of guided reading literacy experts has reviewed and leveled the book to
ensure readers pull ahead and experience success.

Lerner Publications
An imprint of Lerner Publishing Group, Inc.
241 First Avenue North
Minneapolis, MN 55401 USA

For reading levels and more information, look up this title at www.lernerbooks.com.

Main body text set in Memphis Pro 24/39
Typeface provided by Linotype.

Photo Acknowledgments
The images in this book are used with the permission of: © Maartje van Caspel/iStockphoto, p. 3;
© SDI Productions/iStockphoto, pp. 4–5; © Paul Bradbury/iStockphoto, pp. 6–7, 16 (apple); © Ann
in the uk/Shutterstock Images, pp. 8–9, 16 (toast); © wojciech_gajda/iStockphoto, pp. 10–11, 16
(carrots); © kali9/iStockphoto, pp. 12–13; © monkeybusinessimages/iStockphoto, pp. 14–15.

Front cover: © SolStock/iStockphoto

Library of Congress Cataloging-in-Publication Data

Names: Peters, Katie, author.
Title: We all need food / Katie Peters ; GRL Consultant Diane Craig, Certified Literacy Specialist.
Description: Minneapolis : Lerner Publications, [2023] | Series: My world (Pull ahead readers -
    nonfiction) | Audience: Ages 4–7 | Audience: Grades K–1 | Summary: "Carefully leveled text
    and full-color photographs invite readers to explore the foods people eat. Pairs with the
    fiction book, Making Roti"— Provided by publisher.
Identifiers: LCCN 2022006353 (print) | LCCN 2022006354 (ebook) | ISBN 9781728475950
    (library binding) | ISBN 9781728478876 (paperback) | ISBN 9781728483948 (ebook)
Subjects: LCSH: Food—Juvenile literature.
Classification: LCC TX355 .P385 2023 (print) | LCC TX355 (ebook) | DDC 641.3—dc23/
    eng/20220607

LC record available at https://lccn.loc.gov/2022006353
LC ebook record available at https://lccn.loc.gov/2022006354

Manufactured in the United States of America
1 – CG – 12/15/22

Table of Contents

We All Need Food

Everyone needs food to live.

We eat fruit. I like apples.

We eat bread. I like toast.

My family eats vegetables.
I like carrots.

My family eats meat.
I like hot dogs.

What foods do you eat?

What are your favorite foods?

Did You See It?

apple

carrots

toast

Index